MW00782654

We found *Preventing Marriage Meltdown* to be very positive and practical advice based on God's word. It is very useful for sustaining a healthy and vibrant marriage." Loved *Preventing Marriage Meltdown*, especially this, "You can stop forgiving each other when God has stopped forgiving you." And, "Too often, however, when we say we forgive, we have removed the offense from our inbox to our saved file, knowing we can bring it back out for another argument."

Kathy and Robert Bennett

Marriage design or marriage decline. Dr. Caton tells us the potential for both in quite simple and plain truth. Every husband and wife whose marriage is in trouble should spend some time reading and studying the principles laid out in this book.

Dennis and Sharon George

In his introduction, John Mark confesses: "I am a realist, and I know marriage is tough work." Presented in an easy-to-read format, *Preventing Marriage Meltdown* successfully balances biblical truth and practical wisdom for marriages across the spectrum.

Beau Landers

We all have needs and most of us enter into marriage with expectations of what marriage will do for us. Chapter 2 was a great reminder that recognizing your spouse's needs as more important than your own is the type of sacrifice that God honors and blesses in a marriage.

Sandra Dennis

This will be one of my go-to resources for young families. Every married and soon-to-be married couple will benefit from Marriage Meltdown. John Mark expertly presents God's incredible design for marriage and provides practical insights on how God intends for marriages to not only survive but to regularly revive and thrive.

Dave and Sue Marsh

PREVENTING
MARRIAGE
MELTDOWN

PREVENTING
MARRIAGE MELTDOWN

John Mark Caton, Ph.D

Optasia Books
An Imprint of

Bold Vision Books
PO Box 2011
Friendswood, Texas 77549

ISBN #978-0-997-851-4-5-8
LCCN# 2017-932234

Cover Art by Kenny Courtenay

Interior design by *k*ae Creative Solutions

Published in the United States of America.

Bold Vision Books
PO Box 2011
Friendswood, Texas 77549

Optasia Books is an imprint of Bold Vision Books

Dedication

To my children
Jace

Jordan

Jensyn

Jarrett

For the lessons you teach mom and me every day.

And

To my mom, Donnie Caton for the example of godly parenting and a strong, real marriage, for showing strength with the loss of Dad, and for being the best Mom and Grandmother.

Table of Contents

Acknowledgments

Many thanks to my Cottonwood Creek staff for encouraging me to push myself as a pastor, author, husband, father, and friend.

To Jeana, my wife, best friend, editor, and partner in ministry. Thank you for the hours you spent transcribing my sermons on marriage into the base text for this book. For editing and formatting and encouraging me to write. Thank you for a marriage that is real and a life that is rewarding. You are my example of hard-work and dedication. I love you.

Introduction

Both men and women today see marriage not as a way of creating character and community but as a way to reach personal life goals. They are looking for a marriage partner who will "fulfill their emotional, sexual, and spiritual desires." And that creates an extreme idealism that in turn leads to a deep pessimism that you will ever find the right person to marry.
~Tim Keller

Marriages across America are in trouble today. Sadly, Christian marriages are no exception. Research shows that 40 to 50 percent of first-time marriages in the United States end up in divorce. For second and third-time marriages, the rate is perhaps even higher. For Christians, that number is lower but still a troubling 32 percent.[1]

A bride and groom standing at the marriage altar are thinking about the excitement of their honeymoon, the thrill of a life together, and the joy of having kids someday. Rarely do they realize the challenges they will face.

I am not a pessimist when it comes to marriage because a marriage done God's way is amazing. There is nothing like it. I am a realist, and I know marriage is tough work. No one stands at the altar thinking, *Maybe in eight years we'll have nothing in common and get a divorce.*

Brides and grooms don't usually say, "I hope I feel this happy two years from now." Most weddings are filled with optimism and cheerfulness,

---

1   The Barna Group, "New Marriage and Divorce Statistics Released," March 31, 2008, *Barna: www.barna.com/research/new-marriage-and-divorce-statistics-released/#.V8jINZgrLlV* (September 1, 2016); and American Psychological Association, "Marriage and Divorce," www.apa.org/topics/divorce/ (September 1, 2016).

but some wedding couples say their vows while believing it's the first step toward fixing their spouse or helping them grow up. Those couples are on their way to a meltdown.

No marriage is immune to the challenges and struggles that accompany the words, "I do." Every marriage deals with the tensions and pressures that come when two lives join together under one roof. If you have been married for any time at all, I can hear you saying a hearty amen, which is why I have written this book.

Whether you have been married for two days or two decades, your marriage takes work. You must understand how to steer your marriage toward success, how to navigate around the landmines that threaten to destroy your marriage, and how to refresh, renew, and revitalize your relationship with your wonderful man or woman.

Maybe your marriage has captured the magic. People say about you, "I wish I had what they have. I do not know what it is, but you two seem in tune. You work together. You love each other. Your marriage is awesome." If so, this book can remind you how to keep your marriage strong.

Or your marriage may once have had the magic, but now you have lost it. You think, *I just wish we could go back to the sweetness of our early relationship.* If so, I hope this book will help rekindle the magic.

Some of you are beginning the marriage journey. You want to succeed and find that special magic. If so, this book will help your marriage flourish.

Ben Hogan was one of the greatest golfers of all time. Early in his career, Ben thought that the golf swing was about executing a thousand actions perfectly. Later he wrote in his book, *Five Lessons on Golf,* about how he discovered that golf is about doing five fundamental movements well. He began to loosen up and play better when he discovered and applied those five skills.

Like Ben Hogan, many of us think a good marriage requires executing a thousand different actions perfectly. However, To have a truly awesome marriage follow five fundamental guidelines.

- Make God and biblical principles the center of your marriage.

- Let the differences between you and your spouse make your relationship stronger.

- Learn to resolve conflict quickly.

- Forgive constantly.

- Refresh, renew, and revitalize your marriage often.

These five essentials will build a holy and happy marriage—a dream within a dream.

So as you read on, my prayer is that God will use these principles from the truths of His Word to help you build a marriage that shines with the light of Christ instead of melting down—the kind of marriage that will bring you the satisfaction and reward your heart so desperately desires. If you need more incentive to read on look no further than to this quote from Zig Ziglar.

"People who have good relationships at home are more effective in the marketplace."
~Zig Ziglar

John Mark Caton

Chapter 1

The Design of a Marriage That Lasts

Okay, here's how to do relationships—be kind to one another, tenderhearted, forgiving one another, just as God, in Christ, also has forgiven you.
~Chip Ingram

Make God and Biblical Principles the Center of Your Marriage

The Lord God said, "It is not good for the man to be alone. I will make a helper suitable for him." Now the Lord God had formed out of the ground all the wild animals and all the birds in the sky. He brought them to the man to see what he would name them; and whatever the man called each living creature, that was its name. So the man gave names to all the livestock, the birds in the sky and all the wild animals. But for Adam no suitable helper was found. So the Lord God caused the man to fall into a deep sleep; and while he was sleeping, he took one of the man's ribs and then closed up the place with flesh. Then the Lord God made a woman from the rib he had taken out of the man, and he brought her to the man. The man said, "This is now bone of my bones and flesh of my flesh; she shall be called 'woman,' for she was taken out of man." That is why a man leaves

his father and mother and is united to his
wife, and they become one flesh. Adam and
his wife were both naked, and they felt no shame
(Genesis 2:18–25 NIV).

I praise God that one day He answered my prayer for a wife, and I married the perfect woman for me. But our marriage—like all marriages—has gone through difficult times. Jeana's mom went through a long battle with cancer which caused us to be apart many weekends while Jeana was in Houston with her mother. My brother committed suicide and I did not handle it well. The church grew in amazing ways and it seemed like I worked seven days a week twenty-four hours a day. During that time, we had four kids who all became very active in sports, and I added a Ph.D. to my educational achievements. In other words, we were busy, stretched, stressed, and drowning at times. We have had those moments when our love has been tested, and we navigated some difficult waters. However, our marriage has never been stronger or sweeter than it is today because we chose not to quit and not turn on each other.

My heart breaks when I hear about marriages ending in divorce court. How sad that one-third of Christian marriages and up to half of all U.S. marriages end in divorce. Several studies over the past decade have revealed disturbing effects on children burdened by divorce. Higher risks of smoking, stroke, illness, a propensity to crime, and the likelihood of getting divorced themselves all await the children of divorced parents.[2] The marriage bond has not always been so weak. Marriage meltdown is not God's design or desire.

The Weakening of Marriage

In 1970, the divorce rate began to go up, and for the next fifteen years, it continued going up until leveling off at its current rate. What took place in 1970 to increase the divorce rate? It actually happened the year before.

2   Lauren Hansen, "9 negative effects divorce reportedly has on children," March 28, 2013, *The Week: theweek.com/articles/466107/9-negative-effects-divorce-reportedly-children* (September 8, 2016).

In 1969, the Family Law Act was passed in California, which was the first law in the United States that allowed someone to get a divorce for no stated reason. If you wanted a divorce before 1969, you were required to prove adultery, abuse, or that you lived in an unsafe environment. If you could not prove any of these conditions before a judge, you were not granted a divorce. Instead, you were told to fix your marriage because the court believed it could be fixed.

Starting in 1969, state after state passed "No Fault Divorce" laws. These new statutes allowed a spouse to go before the court saying, "I do not like him." Or "I do not like her." Then a divorce would be granted.

Marriage is also declining for other reasons. More people are choosing to live together. They want the benefits of marriage without its entanglements. More people are waiting until they are older to get married (and I do not think this is necessarily a bad thing).

Also, our popular culture is attacking marriage. God-honoring marriage suffers constant attack from opinion-makers in our society. Hollywood will not encourage you to stay married or find excitement in your marriage. If you are trying to model your marriage after anything on TV or in movies, you are in for trouble because all too often the marriages of Hollywood couples end for irreconcilable differences and the celebrities joke about how many times they've been married and divorced.

In June 2010, *Newsweek* published an article by Jessica Bennett and Jesse Ellison arguing against marriage. They claimed that though marriage used to make sense, it no longer does because most, if not all, of the benefits of marriage can be found without any marital commitment. Women have the rights, education, and freedom to live alone, and both men and women can have casual sexual relationships. The authors maintain that single Americans have personal advantages by avoiding marriage.[3]

---

3   Jessica Bennett and Jesse Ellison, "The Case Against Marriage," *Newsweek: www.newsweek.com/case-against-marriage-73045*

Thirty years ago, therapist Carl Rodgers pegged our culture. In his book, *Becoming Partners* (notice it was not titled, *Getting Married*), he wrote,

> To me, it seems we are living in an important and uncertain age. If 50 percent of Ford or General Motors cars fell apart within the early part of their lifetime as automobiles, drastic steps would be taken to change them. We have no such organized way of dealing with our social institution, so people are groping more or less blindly to find alternatives to marriage. Living together without marriage, living in communes, serial monogamy, the women's liberation movement, new divorce laws which do away with the concept of anyone's guilt, these are all groping toward some new form of man/woman or man/ other relationship.

His words were written thirty years ago and today our courts have redefined marriage. Traditional marriage is under attack. Your marriage is under attack, but honestly, this is not a new phenomenon.

In first century Judaism, divorce was a much-debated topic. The Pharisees who were the religious leaders of Jesus day were divided into two camps as to what constituted a legitimate divorce. One group who was lead by a Pharisee named Hillel, argued that a man could divorce his wife for any trivial reason. The idea was that a wife was to please her husband in every way. When the wife no longer pleased the husband he was free to divorce for even very trivial offenses like the burning of a meal.

The other more conservative faction of Pharisees was led by a teacher named *Shammai*. His teachings held that a man was only allowed to divorce his wife for some sort of sexual impurity. This might sound more biblical, but it wasn't at all. Because this more conservative group while limiting divorce to a sexual sin did not allow for the possibility of forgiveness and reconciliation. Instead, if sexual impurity was in fact discovered, divorce was not simply an option, it was a mandate.

So even in Jesus day, God's design for marriage was under attack. Regardless of the century you live in or the place in which you reside, the only way to protect your marriage is to make sure your marriage is built on a solid foundation.

Building on a Solid Foundation

> *God created marriage. No government*
> *subcommittee envisioned it. No social*
> *organization developed it. Marriage was*
> *conceived and born in the mind of God."*
> ~Max Lucado

"Unless the Lord builds the house, its builders labor in vain" (Psalm 127:1 NIV). A solid foundation is the underlying truth of the first principle of avoiding a marital meltdown. Unless God builds your house, you labor in vain. If you want to guarantee success, go to the One who designed marriage. Build your marriage using God's design.

Getting married in a church does not mean you have a Christian marriage. Attending church occasionally or a lot does not mean you have a Christian marriage. In fact, the label Christian doesn't reduce your chances of divorce. However, active and committed Christians experience drastically reduced divorce rates compared with the general population. Glenn Stanton noted several important statistics about active and committed Christians.

People who are serious about their faith have a divorce rate markedly lower than the general population. The factor making the most difference is religious commitment and practice.
Couples who generally take their faith seriously by regularly attending church, reading their Bibles, and praying enjoy significantly lower divorce rates than those who are mere church members, the general public, and unbelievers.

Whether young or old, male or female, low-income or not, those who said they were more religious reported higher levels of commitment to their partners, higher levels of marital satisfaction, less talk about divorce, and lower levels of negative interaction with their mate.[4]

In their book, *Marriage in Light of Forever*, Francis and Lisa Chan try to put a corrective balance on marriage talk. "We need to remember that the goal of marriage isn't mere happiness. It's possible to have a happy and worthless marriage." They say, "It's not that God doesn't want us to be happy. In fact, surrendering to a kingdom-first mindset actually brings us greater fulfillment. When we seek His mission together, greater union with each other becomes the byproduct. Jesus came that we could have life to the full."[5]

Identifying myself as Christian without putting my faith into action does not protect my marriage. The only effective way to enjoy and shield marriage from divorce is to be active and committed to our faith. Committed Christians don't have problem-free marriages, but an active and growing faith allows couples to cope with and solve their problems better. A husband and wife who live as God desires, even when it is hard, will enjoy marriage more and the marriage will not end in divorce.

It takes two! Both the husband and the wife must be willing to commit completely to the marriage. Reread the Psalm again, "Unless the Lord builds the house, its *builders* labor in vain" (Psalm 127:1) [emphasis added]. Notice the word is plural, not singular. It takes both builders in a marriage.

Let's look back to the beginning in Genesis 2:18–25. This passage takes us to the Garden of Eden, before sin entered the world, when God, as the architect of marriage, put the design for marriage together.

---

4   Glenn Stanton, "Fact Checker: Divorce Rate Among Christians," September 25, 2012, *The Gospel Coalition:* www.thegospelcoalition.org/article/fact-checker-divorce-rate-among-christians (September 1, 2016).
5   Francis and Lisa Chan, "Marriage in Light of Forever," ed. Matt Smethurst, December 18, 2014, *The Gospel Coalition:* www.thegospelcoalition.org/article/marriage-in-light-forever (September 8, 2016).

God's Design for Marriage

Notice that the first statement is, "The Lord God said, 'It is not good for the man to be alone.'" You might want to underline that statement in your Bible.

God created the world and all that was in the world and said it was good, but this moment is the first time He said that something was not good. It was not good for man to be alone. God created us to be relational beings.

As God considered how to solve the problem, He said, "I will make a helper suitable for him" (Genesis 2:18 NIV).

> Now the Lord God had formed out of the ground all the wild animals and all the birds in the sky. He brought them to the man to see what he would name them; and whatever the man called each living creature, that was its name. So the man gave names to all the livestock, the birds in the sky and all the wild animals. But for Adam no suitable helper was found. So the Lord God caused the man to fall into a deep sleep; and while he was sleeping, he took one of the man's ribs and then closed up the place with flesh. Then the Lord God made a woman from the rib he had taken out of the man, and he brought her to the man.

I do not believe our English text expresses this event with the same beauty and excitement that we would imagine for such an event. Adam, who has seen all the cows, pigs, birds, and other animals parading in front of him so he could give them name after name, falls into a deep sleep. And when God awakens Adam, Eve is standing before him. Somehow I do not picture Adam coolly saying, "This is now bone of my bones, flesh of my flesh." Surely he said something like, "Wow! Do you see her?"

Then God instructed the two about marriage. "Therefore shall a man leave his father and his mother, and shall cleave unto his wife: and they shall be one flesh. And they were both naked, the man and his wife, and were not ashamed" (Genesis 2:24–25 KJV). In these verses, we are given the essentials for a husband and wife to build a solid and lasting relationship. The essentials of leaving and cleaving are where a great marriage starts.

Leaving

The first word for building a great marriage is *leaving*. That word leave means to depart from permanently. *Leaving* is essential for a marriage built according to God's design.

1. Leave Your Parents.

Every new couple should establish a new home and not be dependent on parents financially, emotionally, or relationally. New couples should deal with your own conflicts and build your relationship on kindness, understanding, and forgiveness. Commit to staying together and working through the challenges and demands of your new life without the safety net or threat of returning back to mother and father.

If you are parents of newlyweds, help that newly married couple by letting them learn responsibility and life-management. Sure you can help in a crisis, but don't constantly and consistently bail the new couple out or interfere. Allow them to *leave and cleave.*

2. Leave Certain Acquaintances

If you are a newly married couple, leave some friends. If, as a single man, your closest friend is a female, your wife has every right to tell you, "I want you to keep your distance from her now that we are married." And husbands, have the right to say the same thing to your wife. Too often I will hear from a divorced husband or wife, "Well, they were in a bike club together." Or, "They jogged together." Or, "They had coffee once in a while." Some acquaintances are not appropriate now that you are married.

If your friends are single, they may not understand your commitment to faithfulness and try to draw you away from your spouse. Ending certain acquaintances is necessary for leaving.

3. Leave Your Problems

When you get married, it is easy to drag your problems into your marriage, but if your marriage is going to thrive, leave those problems behind. If you have had a problem with anger, you must deal with it and leave the problem behind. If you have struggled with an addiction, marriage will not solve it for you. You must get help by casting yourself on Christ and leaving that problem behind you. Deal with issues before you get married. Take steps to do so right away. Unresolved issues only contribute to melted marriages.

Often, the issues that plague people, such as anger, bitterness, and workaholic or perfectionist behavior, reflect an unwillingness to repent of sin or regard your partner as more important than yourself. You may even be unaware of the problem. Stay close to the Lord and read His Word so that His sweet Spirit will deal with these issues in your life. Premarital counseling brings such problems to the forefront and should point the way to a resolution. Prior problems must be left in order to have a strong marriage.

4. Leave Your Past Relationships

Begin the process of leaving your past by never comparing your spouse to a previous boyfriend or girlfriend, either mentally or verbally. If this is not your first marriage, never compare your current husband or wife to a previous husband or wife. Just do not do it. Your marriage will never be as terrific as it could be if you are constantly glancing in the relational rear view mirror of life. It is time to leave your past relationships in the past and move on.

Cleaving

*As God by creation made two of one, so again
by marriage, He made one of two.*
~Thomas Adam

Not only did God say leave, He also commanded that we *cleave* together. The natural question we all have is, "What in the world does it mean to *cleave together?*"

At its core, cleaving carries the idea of a covenant not a contract. There is a big difference. A contract, in its essence, is an agreement between two people who cannot be trusted. It says, "If you fail to fulfill your obligations, here is how I am going to enforce my rights or get out of this obligation."

Marriage is not a contract between two individuals. It is a covenant—a sacred bond—between a man and a woman that they enter into both publicly and in God's presence. Even unbelievers want a church wedding in order to give their wedding vows a sacred quality. Some may argue that a marriage is grounded only in civil law (which can and has been redefined in court) or in church law (which has relevance only to those members who choose to submit to it). But the Bible declares that marriage is a covenant between you and your spouse, a lifestyle into which you have folded your two identities. Both flames are burning on one candle now. You have poured the sand of your lives into each other and cannot be separated.[6]

Unity and Humility

It is easier to define disunity than it is to define unity. If something lacks unity, we say it is a mess, disorderly, or chaos. In sports, when a team isn't playing together it's obvious because of the failure that takes place on the field or the screaming or isolation that takes place on the sidelines. The same can be said for a marriage that lacks unity. However, when a team is unified, the individual players or plays don't necessarily stand out but the product is always positive—a score or a win!

Unity is the combining of all parts into one—agreement, harmony, and accord. In marriage, there is nothing sweeter to watch or experience than the joy of unity

---

6   Andreas J. Köstenberger, and David W. Jones, *God, Marriage, and Family: Rebuilding the Biblical Foundation* (Wheaton, IL: Crossway, 2010), 73–74.

Jesus explained how a good marriage takes place when a husband and wife are united. "'Haven't you read... that at the beginning the Creator 'made them male and female,' and said, 'For this reason a man will leave his father and mother and be united to his wife, and the two will become one flesh?'" (Matthew 19:4–5 NIV).

Gary Thomas said, "Let's teach our children that every good marriage begins with a funeral: the death of our selfish, independent, and arrogant ways." That is unity, but notice unity is not the death of self, it is the death of self-centeredness and self-importance. In other words, when a husband and wife are unified everything they do and say is for the good of the marriage unit.

A unified marriage means that humility trumps *arrogance* and *selfishness*, but humility is hard because self is a formidable foe. It is easy to be selfish because it is natural for us, however, it is hard to be unselfish because it is unnatural. If you have children, you know that you don't have to teach your kids to be selfish. It seems as though they are born that way. Our children seem to learn these words in order "Mom", "Dad", and "Mine." But you didn't have to teach them "Mine." The "mine" habit becomes "ours" when we enter marriage.

To be unselfish means that we think of our mate first. If you think of someone else first, then you have to think of yourself as second—that is humility and it is not easy. Augustine said, "before we can build a tall tower of virtues, we must first dig a deep foundation of humility." Please don't misunderstand. Humility is not thinking less of yourself. Humility does not mean you have to see yourself as the dust on the bottom of your mate's shoes. C. S. Lewis said, "True humility is not thinking less of yourself; it is thinking of yourself less." And if you think of yourself less, then you will think of your mate more.

The Apostle Paul said, "make my joy complete by being like-minded, having the same love, being one in spirit and of one mind" (Philippians 2:2 NIV). The only way to have one love, one spirit, and one mind in marriage is to be unified. So how do we put unity into practice? Think of it this way "One love" means I'm going to love my mate the way I want my mate to love me. "One Spirit" means I'm going to constantly live with a spirit of forgiveness. "One Mind" means I'm going to regularly do what is best for my relationship, not necessarily what is best for me. So true humility and unity mean I care less about being right and more about being loving, forgiving, and unselfish.

If you have been divorced and remarried, don't despair. Instead do everything you can to build a godly, unified marriage. Commit to never go down the path of a broken marriage again. The research I have read says that your best chance for happiness is in the relationship you are in right now. It is not with your next wife or your next husband. It is in the relationship you are in today. So even if you feel like your marriage is in trouble, ask God to put it back together. He is the great healer.

Jesus goes on to say, "So they are no longer two, but one flesh. Therefore, what God has joined together, let no one separate" (Matthew 19:6 NIV). God put you together. Do not let anyone separate you.

Privacy

The next foundational piece of God's design for marriage is the need for privacy. Some elements of marriage are sacred and are no one's business but yours. Let me encourage you with all of my heart to never share marital secrets with your friends or family.

When a marriage partner shares private information with mom or dad or sister or brother or best friend, the result is often explosive because moms, dads, siblings, and friends are not impartial. They choose sides quickly and forgive slowly and animosity or anger begins to smolder.

Marriage is a sacred relationship that requires a high level of privacy within the marriage. By protecting that privacy, you will gain openness with your spouse, which is a vital part of a strong marriage. As a couple, work out problems together in humble reliance on the Lord, keeping most things between the two of you. If there are some things going on in your marriage that you simply must share, I am a strong advocate for our third party counselor who is impartial.

A healthy marriage is a place filled with open and honest communication between the husband and wife. In the first marriage, "Adam and his wife were both naked, and they felt no shame" (Genesis 2:25 NIV). Marriage is the place where you can bare your soul and feel safe, never concerned that one of you will tell a friend who will tell a spouse who will tell another friend. Marriage is the perfect place to share your deepest, darkest fears and get encouragement. In marriage, your failures never become public knowledge. That kind of discretion can only happen when there is a mutual commitment to honoring the privacy of marriage. Only acts of abuse or certain dangerous sins supersede this privacy, but even then, you can usually seek solutions and help confidentially. Establish this simple, but helpful, rule in your marriage: Both public and private marital problems will be handled as privately as possible to bring about real solutions.

Renewal

A successful marriage means falling in love many times, always with the same person!

The final piece of the foundation for a God-designed marriage is that the marriage is a refreshing place. Wives, when your husband comes home, commit to finding ways to refresh him—physically and emotionally by listening and by allowing the fruit of the Spirit to fill your home. Husbands, refresh your wife with kindness and understanding about her frustrations at home and on the job. Look for ways to renew and refresh her.

Marriage is the refreshing and replenishing place for the battles ahead. Home is not the place for domestic fights to begin. Your home is your "pit stop" where you and your spouse get an encouraging tune-up, and when you leave for work the next day, both of you are refueled and refreshed.

As the blueprint is essential to building a new building, God's blueprint allows you to build your marriage and avoid a marital meltdown. The details of each house are different. Some homes are modern; some are traditional; some are colorfully painted; some are brick; some are wood. In the same way, marriages differ—some have two kids; some have six; some couples have busy schedules; some have clear schedules; some are structured and organized; and others seem to go with the flow. Your house is your house; make it great.

Though the specific details may differ, God has given one blueprint that applies to every marriage—so that the marriage will be strong and able to withstand the fiercest storms. But it is your choice. The greatest preacher of all time, Jesus, in the greatest sermon, the Sermon on the Mount, wants you and me to understand that it is our choice. He has given us the blueprint for a marriage that will last.

> Therefore, everyone who hears these words of mine and puts them into practice is like a wise man who built his house on the rock. The rain came down, the streams rose, and the winds blew and beat against that house; yet it did not fall, because it had its foundation on the rock (Matthew 7:24–25 NIV).

Now we must apply those truths. If we practice leaving, cleaving, unity, privacy, and renewal, our house will be able to stand against the rains, the floods, and the winds of life. If we choose *not* to put them into practice, the result is failure.

> But everyone who hears these words of mine and does not put them into practice is like a foolish man who built his house on sand. The rain came down, the streams rose, and the winds blew and beat against that house, and it fell with a great crash (Matthew 7:26–27 NIV).

A Marriage Built to Last

> *Marriage is not 50-50. Divorce is 50-50. Marriage has to be 100-100. Marriage isn't dividing everything in half, but giving everything you've got!*
> --Dave Willis

As Jesus told the parable of the two houses built on different foundations, He gives us insight into what it takes to build a marriage that will last. The first insight is in every relationship, there is the potential for two types of builders. One who is wise and one who is foolish. The wise builder listened and followed directions. The fool ignored what was said and ended up in a disastrous situation.

The second insight from Jesus is that there are two foundations. One foundation is the Rock, which is the solid foundation of God's Word. With God's foundation, we understand his design, his purpose, and his plan. The other foundation is the world's foundation—the sand. A sandy foundation shifts and is unstable and eventually collapses.

But there is a problem in this parable, which leads me to the third insight: There is one experience that is guaranteed to hit your marriage. It's going to rain. May I say that again? It is going to rain. Sometimes the rain is just an inconvenient and messy season in life. We are too busy or our priorities are a little mixed up or we have money problems. Other times it rains harder, and we find ourselves less able to function and bogged down in the muck of life. For example, we lack intimacy, lose a job, or a child is in full rebellion. Still others times it rains hard. Hard rains come in the form of an affair, bankruptcy, addiction, abuse, or the diagnosis of a life-changing illness. So remember it is going to rain, and the wind will blow in your marriage at some point. That is why Jesus says, "Hey, do not build on the sand when you have the opportunity to build your house on the rock." [my paraphrase]

Make a commitment today to follow God's design to build a marriage that will last. If you do, your marriage will withstand whatever storm may come your way.

Chapter 2

When Opposites Attract

*On the most elementary level, you do not
have to go to church to be a Christian.
You do not have to go home to be married
either. But in both cases if you do not, you
will have a very poor relationship.*
~R. Kent Hughes

**Allow the differences between you and your
spouse make your relationship stronger.**

For this reason a man will leave his father and
mother and be united to his wife, and the two will
become one flesh. This is a profound mystery—but
I am talking about Christ and the church. However,
each one of you also must love his wife as he loves
himself, and the wife must respect her husband
(Ephesians 5:31–33 NIV).

Men and women are different. You may think that is an obvious
statement, but too many husbands and wives do not live like
they understand this truth.

God created us as different as night and day. When we start dating, it
is those differences that attract us to each other. If we are not careful,
those differences can also cause us to attack each other.

In this chapter, I want to focus on those differences that bring us together, uniting us, encouraging us, and causing us to enjoy each other. Our differences make us interesting to each other. In another chapter, I will show you how they can cause us to attack each other.

Reread Ephesians 5:31–33, which is quoted on the previous page. In these verses, Paul describes the mystery of marriage. A mystery is a profound truth that can be hidden or remain unknown. If we are not careful, we can miss the hidden message of marriage. God created each of us uniquely different. He calls us to minister to each other and to encourage each other in diverse ways.

For instance, notice in the passage at the beginning of this chapter how Paul makes certain we understand that men and women are not the same. We are not interchangeable. We are different in our needs.

A woman's needs do not match a man's needs. We must learn and understand those differences. Paul tells us that the wife needs her husband's "love" and the husband needs "admiration and respect" from his wife.

Several years ago, Dr. Willard Harley, Jr. wrote a book titled *His Needs, Her Needs*. In it, he defines five basic needs of a man and five basic needs of a woman based on his experience counseling couples. It is an excellent book that explains the differences between the needs of men and women.

Dr. Harley realized that traditional marriage counseling techniques that had been effective in the past were no longer effective. He noted that back in the 1940s and 50s, the best marriage counseling took place in the form of directives that stressed commitment, love, and sacrifice. Those directives required a commitment to selflessness. However, after the 1960s the idea of "selflessness" was replaced by "selfishness." Dr. Harley said the "Me Generation" was born. "Selflessness" was not common vocabulary and certainly was not something they valued in relationships.

Beyond the "Me Generation" of married couples rejecting the idea of selflessness in their relationships, Dr. Harley said couples also rejected the idea of unconditional love and commitment. He admitted that at times in his counseling he would come across individuals who were willing to try the selflessness and unconditional love idea but were then left in a state he referred to as "permanently neglected."

As a result of his failure in marriage counseling, he admitted that he was baffled and even decided he was not cut out for the job of marriage counseling, so he stopped all marriage counseling for a while. Later, he relaunched his passion for marriage counseling and changed his focus and research. In doing so Dr. Harley realized that every man and every woman had what he called a "Love Bank." In his analogy, every person has an individual account in their mate's Love Bank. Every encounter with that person is either a positive or negative. Positive interactions were like deposits in the Love Bank while negative interactions were like withdrawals from the Love Bank. Dr. Harley then studied what constituted a deposit into the love bank for husbands and what constituted a deposit for wives.

In his study, Dr. Harley determined that every man has five basic needs and every woman has five essential needs. As he added these principles to his counseling practice, his success rate as a marriage counselor began to soar. The core of his counseling was to challenge each husband to stop looking at himself and start meeting the needs of his wife which were effectively making deposits in her Love Bank. He challenged each wife to stop focusing on her needs and start meeting the needs of her husband which were deposits to her Love Bank.

Let's take a look at the needs Dr. Harley identified. Consider how you might apply these principles to your marriage.

The Needs of Husbands

Let the wife make the husband glad
he came home and let the husband
make the wife sorry to see him leave.
~Martin Luther

1. Personal Admiration

That word admiration means to have a feeling of wonder, pleasure or approval for someone. Every husband needs to know he is admired by his wife. Your husband needs a cheerleader. What do cheerleaders do? They stand on the sidelines and cheer the team on no matter the situation. Ladies, your husband needs your admiration and encouragement. He needs you to acknowledge and celebrate his successes. He needs your loyalty and support when difficulty arises. In the latter part of Ephesians 5:33, Paul said, "The wife must respect her husband." The essence of the word *respect* is to admire. You must admire, respect, and honor your husband not necessarily because he deserves it but because he "needs" it. As Dr. Harvey says, "Behind every man should be an admiring wife. A man simply thrives on a woman's admiration." If the wife doesn't admire and respect her husband she leaves him longing for and vulnerable to the admiration and respect of someone else.

2. Recreational Companionship

A man needs his wife to approve of his recreational choices and participate where she can. If your husband loves sports, prepare a great game day spread and watch the game with him. "The couple that plays together," Dr. Harley says, "stays together."

My wife, Jeana, has been hunting with me on very few occasions, but she supports my hunting expeditions because she knows I love it. The first time she went hunting with me was right after we were married. We thought we would do a little bit of bonding. Just before we got to the hunting area, we pulled into McDonald's for an early dinner. We then went out to the deer stand, got settled in. I thought we were in great shape. But Jeana had ordered a big Coke with dinner and when we got still she said, "I have got to go to the bathroom."

I said, "Well, that is just tough. You should have thought about that before we got into the deer stand."

And she said, "You are kidding me?"

And I said, "If you get out, we might as well go home."

She said, "really? How long do I have to wait?"

Then I said, "When the sun goes down, you can get out." So we sat. Then Jeana started tapping her fingers on the stand. I said, "You cannot do that."

"Can we talk?" she said.

"No, we cannot talk."

We were both glad when the sun went down that night. But as I look back, even with the challenges of that day, it was great to just hang out. We still laugh about that experience today and she gave me permission to share it in this book. I appreciated her effort to join in the recreation I enjoyed.

3. Domestic Support

Solomon said, "Better to live on a corner of the roof than share a house with a quarrelsome wife" (Proverbs 21:9 NIV). Men need domestic tranquility or serenity. In other words, when a man comes home from work, he needs to enter a home of serenity, support, and encouragement. The popularity of happy hour came about because husbands needed a transition from war at the office and war at home. Happy hour allows him to slip off to a bar for a few drinks or a few snacks before he faces the family battle. Wives, I recommend you create an environment of serenity and encouragement. When he walks through the door, don't lash out at him or unload your problems on him without giving him a chance to breathe. He needs a calm structure that does not require his constant attention. He needs an encouraging environment that will reward his participation, not drain his energies.

4. Physical Attractiveness

One of a husband's needs is a physically attractive wife. God created men that way, but attractive doesn't simply have to do with appearance.

That word attractive means providing pleasure, delight and being pleasing. Peter gives some great advice on this point in the context of a wife being attractive to her unbelieving husband.

> Your beauty should not come from outward
> adornment, such as elaborate hairstyles and the
> wearing of gold jewelry or fine clothes. Rather,
> it should be that of your inner self, the unfading
> beauty of a gentle and quiet spirit, which is of
> great worth in God's sight. For this is the way the
> holy women of the past who put their hope
> in God used to adorn themselves. They
> submitted themselves to their own husbands
> (1 Peter 3:3–5 NIV).

I have heard some preachers use this passage to say that women should not wear jewelry or makeup or fine clothes. That is not the message Peter is teaching. He says outward beauty pales in comparison to inward beauty. Godly character and moral virtue are what make a woman most attractive. Inward beauty always radiates outward making the wife more attractive. The opposite is also true. Inward unpleasantness always radiates outward and can diminish outward beauty.

When a man or a woman accepts lies about his or her identity in Christ, the soul is weakened. The person who thinks they do not amount to anything or that they don't matter to anyone is practicing habits that will make them unattractive. By trusting in the Lord, by building her heart on Christ's firm foundation, a woman will become more beautiful as she grows in Christ. On the flip side, a naturally beautiful person becomes less attractive through bitterness, jealousy, anger and pride.

Husbands want to be continually attracted to their wives. Ladies trust me they want that. So ladies, take care of your outward appearance, but also remember Peter's words. Cultivate an inner beauty that does not fade with age and you will grow in physical attractiveness throughout your life.

5. Physical Intimacy

The fifth essential need of a husband is physical intimacy. Dr. Harley believes this is the number one need of a man. "That is why a man leaves his father and mother and is united to his wife, and they become one flesh" (Genesis 2:24 NIV). Physical intimacy is a great need for every husband. This need is so important that the apostle Paul addresses it in his first letter to the church at Corinth.

> But since sexual immorality is occurring, each man should have sexual relations with his own wife, and each woman with her own husband. The husband should fulfill his marital duty to his wife, and likewise the wife to her husband. The wife does not have authority over her own body but yields it to her husband. In the same way, the husband does not have authority over his own body but yields it to his wife. Do not deprive each other except perhaps by mutual consent and for a time, so that you may devote yourselves to prayer. Then come together again so that Satan will not tempt you because of your lack of self-control
> (1 Corinthians 7:2–5 NIV).

Sex is a gift from God. Scripture is clear that God designed sex to be freely enjoyed within the confines of a marriage relationship. God designed our bodies in an original and perfect way to bring the husband and wife into physical harmony through sexual intimacy. However, even the greatest gifts can be spoiled or misused. If we are not careful, this wonderful act of intimacy, which was given for our benefit, can become a shackle that hinders us from enjoying marriage fully.

Paul offers two clear points of wisdom that relate to physical intimacy in marriage. First, our bodies are not our own but are jointly owned by our spouse, which naturally conveys the ideas of right and privilege. Further, Paul asserts that, if couples choose not to come together in intimacy, they only do so upon mutual consent. Then after that time of mutual consent is over, they should come back together so that

Satan would not be able to gain a foothold through sexual temptation. Ladies, please do not use sex or the withholding of it as a tool to vent your anger or to teach your husband a lesson. Honestly, if you do, you are begging for trouble. Hear Paul's warning at the opening of this passage clearly—there is much immorality out there.

The Needs of Wives

The most important thing a father can do
for his children is to love their mother.
~Henry Ward Beecher

1. Family Commitment

Every wife needs to be assured of her husband's commitment to her and the family. She wants to know the family you have together is the husband's number one priority. You cannot work sixty hours a week, leaving the house at 6:00 am in the morning and getting home at 7:00 or 8:00 at night, have a golf game scheduled at 8:00 on Saturday morning, and a ballgame that night, and then let her take the kids to church because you are too tired. That behavior does not demonstrate the priority of the family. In fact, it shows the opposite. In Ephesians 5:33 (NIV), Paul tells men, "Each one of you also must love his wife as he loves himself." One of the ways you love your wife is to love your family and make it a priority by spending time with them, lots of time with them.

2. Real Conversation

Wives need real, honest-to-goodness communication. Rich interaction requires time, meaning husbands must listen carefully and talk in complete sentences. Difficult, I know, but guys conversation is something your wife needs. I have learned that my wife needs time to talk—real conversation without distractions such as TV or sports or the newspaper. She needs to know what is going on in my life and to let me know what is going on in her life.

When a wife describes her feelings or a difficult situation, men open the toolbox to find a way to fix the problem. Men seem to want to get to the point and find a solution. And when we do, the wife typically says, "Never mind." When my wife says, "Never mind," I know that I have missed something or I'm not valuing the topic as much as she does. I realize pretty quickly, I had better begin to pay attention and engage in real conversation or risk a cold shoulder the rest of the evening.

Romans 12:15 (NIV) provides a great pattern for men to use when having real conversation with wives. "Rejoice with those who rejoice; mourn with those who mourn." Men, do not try to fix her. If she is sharing her day, share in her day. If she is rejoicing, rejoice and give her an ATTAGIRL! If she is crying, hug her while she cries. In the movie, *A League of Their Own* Tom Hanks spoke to one of the female players and said "there's no crying in baseball" and he was right.

However, life isn't baseball, and there is crying in life. So, guys when your wife is struggling, support her through the difficult time without trying to fix the problem. Listen, support, encourage, and affirm her.

3. Domestic Security

While men need support and peacefulness, women need security—primarily financial security. A recent article about dating and relationships on the website Statistic Brain stated that 88% of women felt that "money was very important in a relationship." Why is money important? Because money provides security and probably means a stable job. That is domestic security.

In Colossians 3:23 (NIV), we are told, "Whatever you do, work at it with all your heart." Men, our wives need to know that we are working as hard as we can to provide for the family. The last thing your wife needs is for you to say, "Honey, I got mad at the boss today and quit my job and I have no plan for our future." Guys, if you do that you might be thinking I showed the boss, but your wife will think her world is crashing down. She needs financial and domestic security. You don't have to be the richest man in the world, but work hard and earn the best living you can in order to provide domestic security for your wife and family. She needs to know that you go to work every day because you want to support her and the family.

4. Honesty and Openness

Your wife needs to share in the deepest part your life so be open and honest about the struggles you encounter. Men tend to get quiet because of some of the problems in life and because men do not especially want women to worry or be concerned, they go into a cave until the problem is figured out. If you are single, solving problems in isolations is fine but if you are married that can cause problems.

When a wife sees her husband isolating himself, she sees it as withdrawal from her and the family; a distance between them may start to develop. She may worry, feel rejected and even lack trust when she is pushed out of her man's cave. The distance emotionally, physically and relationally between the husband and wife will grow.

Openness and honesty require a husband to tell his wife about his problems. The wife may or may not be able to help solve the problem, but simply letting her know what is occupying your thoughts right now will actually eliminate the lack of trust or feeling of rejection. You may want to protect her, but when she knows your inner struggle and your difficult situations, she will believe in you and become your best advocate and supporter.

Peter said, "Husbands, in the same way be considerate as you live with your wives, and treat them with respect as the weaker partner and as heirs with you of the gracious gift of life, so that nothing will hinder your prayers" (1 Peter 3:7 NIV). The accurate translation of the word *considerate* is "according to knowledge." Do not deceive her instead give her the knowledge of what is going on. Live with her as an understanding partner, someone who knows you and the details of your life.

Peter also said to treat her with respect "as the weaker partner." She is like the fine china, and as a man, you are the everyday dishes. *Weaker* does not mean intellectually or emotionally weaker. It does not mean more frail than her husband morally or spiritually. From the context of Peter's letter, the word refers to a woman's physical strength and perhaps voice in a particular society. So in treating her respectfully as a weaker partner, you do not want to dominate her physically or minimize her voice in your life. When writing on 1 Peter 3:7, scholar Karen Jobes said, "Peter teaches that men whose authority runs roughshod over their women, even with society's full approval, will not be heard by God."[7]

Peter also said that your wife is an heir with you "of the gracious gift of life." She is a joint heir. As a joint heir, she has a need for you to share openly and honestly.

5. Relational Affection

Affection means a fond attachment, devotion or love. Relational affection means speaking kindly to the wife, holding hands, hugging, and kissing. That is what your wife needs from you. She needs a kind word, a smile, a kiss and a hug. She wants to hold your hand at a ball game. She needs those demonstrations of relational affection. The Apostle Paul alludes to this in Colossians 3:19 (NIV), "Husbands, love your wives and do not be harsh with them." Your wife is like fine china. She is soft, precious, and sweet. She needs the soft touches verbally and emotionally that will benefit your relationship greatly.

As you can see from these lists of needs, men and women are different by God's design. When we understand each other's needs, we build strong marriages that will help prevent marital meltdown.

Men, your marriage is not about you. It is about her. Women, your marriage is not about you, it is about him. I truly believe that if husbands and wives would spend more time trying to make deposits in their mates Love Bank marital satisfaction would soar. You might think, *You do not*

---

7   Karen H. Jobes, *1 Peter*, ed. Robert W. Yarbrough and Robert H. Stein, *Baker Exegetical Commentary on the New Testament* (Grand Rapids, MI: Baker Academic, 2005), 209.

know my spouse. You are right, I don't. But I know God's design for marriage. If you will live according to God's design and work together to meet each other's needs as much as possible, God will bless your marriage.

Chapter 3

When Opposites Attack

*Countless mistakes in marriage, parenting,
ministry, and other relationships are failures to
balance grace and truth. Sometimes we neglect
both. Often we choose one over the other.*
~Randy Alcorn

Learn to Resolve Conflict

If a house is divided against
itself, that house cannot stand
(Mark 3:25 NIV).

Any builder will tell you the most important part of a building is the foundation. If we are not careful in our marriage, we can create an unstable foundation.

Most often I have seen shaky foundations created because of conflict. We take verbal jabs at each other. We lace our conversation with sarcasm that is not funny but intended to hurt. Sarcasm is defined as harsh or bitter derision. Sarcasm from time to time might get a chuckle, but if there is no caring and loving conversation it will eventually shake the core of your marriage.

Every marriage will have conflict of some sort because you and your spouse are completely different people. It is how you handle and deal with the conflict that is important. Jesus makes it clear in the verse

44

quoted above, "If the house is divided against itself, that house cannot stand."

So, I want to deal directly with the topic of conflict. Conflict is inevitable, but how far you let it go before it begins to disturb or destroy you is the key to preventing marital meltdown. When conflict erupts you immediately have choices. Will you settle the dispute quickly? Will you let it rage out of proportion to the actual problem? Or will you use the battle to hone and sharpen your marriage?

If properly understood and handled, conflict can make you and your marriage better.

The Source of Conflict

> *Many marriages would be better*
> *if the husband and the wife clearly*
> *understood that they are on the same side.*
> *~Zig Ziglar*

We discover the source of conflict when James writes, "What causes fights and quarrels among you? Don't they come from your desires that battle within you?" (James 4:1 NIV). Each of us has selfish desires that battle within us. If you remember in the last chapter, we discovered basic needs of a man and a woman. When those needs go unmet they can then become selfish desires that burn inside us. The problem is those battles within us do not stay inside us, and the way they tend to flesh themselves out most often is in our relationships.

Earlier we looked at Genesis which says, "So God created mankind in His own image, in the image of God He created them; male and female He created them" (Genesis 1:27 NIV). God tells us first that He created men and women differently. Marriage is a lifelong process of overcoming differences and meeting different needs.

Husbands and wives are biologically different. We have wide differences wrapped up in our DNA as human beings and as individual personalities. The two of you come from various families and backgrounds. My wife

45

comes from a sweet, loving, caring family with a father who was the kindest man I have ever met. My dad was a great dad, but he was the son of an alcoholic who beat his wife. We did not hug a lot in my family. But Jeana's family hugs.

Perhaps you came into marriage having dated only one boyfriend or one girlfriend and your relationships were good, but your spouse has a background of difficulty, hardship, and hurt in relationships. These two histories must merge together. Marriage will be a lifelong process of overcoming those experiential, emotional, and personality differences.

Not only that, we come into marriage with different communication styles, varying likes and dislikes, wants and needs. Marriage is indeed a lifelong process of overcoming these divergent details of our past.

One day, Jeana and I sat down together and listed out all our differences. Let me give you just a flavor of the two of us. (And, yes, I have her permission to share these with you.)

One of the greatest differences between Jeana and me is that I am a night owl and she is a morning person. If I see the sunrise, I want to be hunting something. Other than that, I do not care about it that much. However, when the sun goes down, I am energized. That's probably what kept me in trouble most of my life prior to marriage. When we were first married, she was teaching and I was going to seminary and working. Every evening at about 8:30, she went to sleep, but I would be just getting started for the night. After more than twenty-five years of marriage, I'm still a night owl and she is still a morning person.

The alarm clock is another way we are different. I was under the impression you set an alarm clock for when you wanted to get up. If I need to get up at 6:00, I set it for 6:00. But if she wants to get up at 6:00, she sets the alarm for 5:15. That way, she can go through gradual stages of awareness before she actually gets up.

I like it cold, and she likes it warm. When I think it's hot outside, Jeana grabs a jacket. This difference makes for some difficult rides in the car. It is not an uncommon occurrence to this day for Jeana to turn the heat on and I turn it off. I looked away to talk to the kids, and when I looked back, the heat is back on again. I turn it down; she turns it up.

I like my food spicy, she likes hers bland. If I cook chili, I am the only one in the family who can eat it because it is so hot. If she cooks it, everybody eats it and I load it up with jalapeños or Tabasco.

I am loud, and she is quiet.

I like contemporary music. She likes the traditional hymns.

I walk fast, and she walks slowly. If we are going to the mall, my purpose is to get from one end to the other and back again as quickly as we can. She wants to stroll.

I do not have mercy, but my wife is a mercy shower. Spiritual gifts tests reveal that I am an encourager.

I am direct when I speak. Jeana speaks about hard topics with sweetness and kindness.

I will not read fiction, but Jeana loves a good novel, usually one that ends in tears.

After working through this list, we came to a conclusion: We are totally incompatible. We seem to have no reason to be married. In reality, those differences are what excite us about each other. Our differences give us reason to celebrate. We would not be better off if our spouses were just like us.

The real key to a good relationship is what is called the state-of-mind marriage. What does this mean? There are three states of mind that control every marriage. Depending on your state of mind, your marriage could be great or a disaster.

The first state of mind is **togetherness**. When you started dating, you and your spouse were unified in purpose, heartbeat, and conversation. You shared everything as a couple. Words like *we* and *our* and *us* dominated your conversations. *My* rarely found its way to your voice. It was *we*. It was *you*. However, as a marriage progresses the *we* wears off.

Which drives you to the next state. **Conflict**—the state of mind where your differences begin to annoy you, and you begin to verbalize issues that you know you should not. Fighting begins. The nipping turns to snipping, and the snipping turns into an argument, and then the argument turns into the cold shoulder, and the cold shoulder becomes a cold week. And can continue for years.

The third state is **withdrawal**—when you begin to back out of your marriage. You put your relationship in reverse and begin to look at the door. In this state, you move into the ice age of your marriage. It takes time and energy to freeze anything, including your marriage.

Freezing your marriage is a series of choices. Choosing to go to bed mad. Choosing to fight about the unimportant. Refusing to say you are sorry. Making your spouse pay when you are angry. These choices leave your marriage cold and lifeless. It takes time to freeze a marriage and it also takes time to thaw it out.

Paul gives us advice on what will make for a warm relationship. "Finally, brothers and sisters, whatever is true, whatever is noble, whatever is right, whatever is pure, whatever is lovely, whatever is admirable—if anything is excellent or praiseworthy—think about such things" (Philippians 4:8 NIV). This verse is one of the best for marriage counseling.

I cannot tell you how many times I have sat across from a couple that should have a great marriage, but are a wreck because they focused on the wrong things. They followed the progression of these three mindsets—togetherness, conflict, and withdrawal—to the point of giving up on their marriage for irreconcilable differences.

At the early stage of marriage, we practice Philippians 4:8. We focus on the noble, right, pure, lovely, admirable and praiseworthy. That focus is why we said, "I love you." Those thoughts are why we often said *we*. But the longer we are married, it is possible to change focus from the good to the bad. Focus on the negative instead of the positive. What was wrong instead of what was right. Moving the marriage from togetherness to conflict.

When you were dating your spouse, you may have seen some qualities you didn't like, but you thought, "Hey when I put a ring on her finger, I will straighten her up." That was a bad call. We are who we are and with God's help, we can change, but the reality is that most of the time we move from conflict to withdrawal because we have given up on trying to change.

Conflict occurs in every relationship, but there are ways to handle it fairly.

Commit To Kindness And Forgiveness

The first keys to a great marriage are kindness and compassion. You practiced both instinctively when you first married, but over time resentment built up and compassion faded away. Paul wrote, "Be kind and compassionate to one another, forgiving each other, just as in Christ God forgave you" (Ephesians 4:32 NIV).

Another essential for marriage is forgiveness. The word *forgiving* is a participle, and it means *continuing* to forgive each other the same way as God *continues* to forgive you in Christ. Forgiveness is unending no matter what your spouse said or did. You can stop forgiving when God has stopped forgiving you.

Learn to forgive God's way! "For as high as the heavens are above the earth, so great is his love for those who fear him; as far as the east is from the west, so far has he removed our transgressions from us" (Psalm 103:11-12 NIV).

Too often, however, when we say we forgive, we have removed the offense from our inbox to our saved file, knowing we can bring it back out for another argument. If we are to forgive as God forgave us in Christ, we forgive completely and never rehash the offense again.

49

Watch Your Words

Avoid toxic phrases. Statements like *"You're just like your mom/dad" "Of course a man/woman would think that" "If you feel that way, maybe we should get a divorce"* and *"It's your problem, not mine"* as well as words like *always* and *never* are absolutely toxic. By speaking in accusations and absolutes, you open the door to the destruction of your marriage. Avoid specific phrases or topics that you know are hurtful to your mate and everyone has a sensitive topic that when talked about are not constructive. Notice what Paul says, "Do not let any unwholesome talk come out of your mouths, but only what is helpful for building others up according to their needs, that it may benefit those who listen" (Ephesians 4:29 NIV). The word *unwholesome* is a term in the original Greek that means "rotten." It is a grocery term used to describe something in the Greek market that was no longer fit for consumption. They would feed rotten food to the pigs, so Paul says that some words are not even fit for the pigs, and we should not let any of those words come out of our mouths—especially toward our mate. Instead, our words should be "helpful for building up others according to their needs."

We've talked about the needs of husbands and wives. I mentioned that if you get married in order for your mate to meet your needs, you are going to be disappointed and discouraged in your marriage. Instead, approach your marriage with the commitment to meet the needs of your spouse. In counseling sessions, one or both spouses sometimes say, "Well, if he will just start," or, "If she would just." When I hear those kinds of statements, I know that he or she has placed a condition on the willingness to show love to the spouse. There is no conditional clause in the words of Paul. He says our words are "for building others up according to their needs, that it may benefit those who listen."

So commit to watching your words. If you feel you are losing an argument, do not react by pulling out that one phrase you know will dig deeply and hurt your spouse. Watch your words, and pray along with the psalmist, "Set a guard, O Lord, over my mouth; keep watch over the door of my lips" (Psalm 141:3 NASB). Keep watch over your lips' door. Be careful that the words you say do not inflict harm and damage.

Adjust the Volume Down

If you are not careful, if you are not cautious, when you get into a conflict with your mate, you will dial up the volume. A small argument can escalate into a bigger argument, and before you know it, words get louder. Then we say some hurtful words and dial up the volume a little more. Soon you can't remember what you started fighting about and the two of you are yelling at each other. Instead heed the Proverb, "A gentle answer turns away wrath, but a harsh word stirs up anger" (Proverbs 15:1 NASB). A gentle word is a soft word and it turns away wrath and there is no better gentle phrase than to whisper during a disagreement "I love you!"

Do you remember Newton's three laws of motion? His third law of motion states that for every action there is an equal and opposite reaction. In marriage, there are always two forces working together. One spouse fights back when you get into an argument or one spouse is not a fighter—whose basic nature is to back away when there is a disagreement.

Here is the problem when a spouse backs away. The fighter spouse thinks; *I am winning all of these battles.* But the battles are driving the non-fighter spouse away, because he or she can't engage or communicate with you without a fight. One day the non-fighter spouse may walk away, heading in the direction you have been pushing them for a long time. Remember, "A gentle answer turns away wrath, but a harsh word stirs up anger. The tongue of the wise makes knowledge acceptable, But the mouth of the fools spouts folly" (Proverbs 15:1–2 NASB). Turn down the volume. Do not let your conflicts get out of control. Learn to say, "I am sorry," and confess your sins to each other.

Conflict in marriage is inescapable, but we must take steps to repair the rift in your relationship and warm to each other again. Scripture shows us how to move from withdrawal to togetherness.

The Solution to Conflict

*To solve a marriage problem, you have to talk with
each other about it, choosing wisely the time and place.
But when accusations and lengthy speeches of
defense fill the dialogue, the partners are not
talking to each other but past each other. Take
care to listen more than you speak. If you still
can't agree on a solution, consider asking a third
party, without a vested interest, to mediate.*
~R.C. Sproul

Be Honest About Your Shortcomings

Why do you look at the speck of sawdust in your
brother's eye and pay no attention to the plank in
your own eye? How can you say to your brother,
"Let me take the speck out of your eye," when
all the time there is a plank in your own eye?
You hypocrite, first take the plank out of
your own eye, and then you will see clearly to
remove the speck from your brother's eye
(Matthew 7:3–5 NIV).

I want to direct this thought toward husbands because it is easy for us
to complain when we come home. We do this, in part, because in our
jobs we spend the day identifying and solving problems. Still, in that
workplace mindset, we naturally come home and begin finding fault
with our home and our wife.

When we behave this way, we are being hypocrites, because each of us
has such large planks in our own lives, too. We demand from our wives
something that we are not demanding of ourselves.

We must first examine ourselves and practice plank removal realizing
that none of us are perfect. We must also be willing to acknowledge
those imperfections to our mate. When our spouse sees honesty and

vulnerability, he or she will be more inclined to practice his or her own plank removal. Being honest about shortcomings changes the atmosphere in the home.

Change Your Focus

> Then make my joy complete by being like-mind-ed, having the same love, being one in spirit and of one mind. Do nothing out of selfish ambition or vain conceit. Rather, in humility value others above yourselves, not looking to your own interests but each of you to the interests of the others (Philippians 2:2-4 NIV).

Paul gives us a good antidote for wrong focus in Philippians. Marital joy is enhanced when a couple is like-minded—what I call a "togetherness mind." A mindset that sees marriage as about *us,* not about *me.* This mindset of togetherness expresses itself by having the same love for each other, being one in spirit and purpose—doing "nothing out of selfish ambition or vain conceit." In other words, you don't spell "marriage" with "I, me, mine."

Having such a mindset will make your marriage more enjoyable, and it will even allow you to live longer. Study after study shows that happily married people live longer than people who have not been happily married. I do not believe anybody goes into a marriage wanting a bad marriage. That is why I encourage singles, if I sense that they are trying to drive to the altar too quickly, to take it more slowly. A bad marriage is worse than bad singleness. A good marriage is phenomenal. I want to encourage you, if you are single, do not go forward until you are certain that the relationship is what God has for you.

Make Peace Quickly

> *Love me when I least deserve it because*
> *that is when I really need it.*
> ~Swedish Proverb

> Therefore, if you are offering your gift at the
> altar and there remember that your brother or
> sister has something against you, leave your gift
> there in front of the altar. First go and be recon-
> ciled to them; then come and offer your gift
> (Matthew 5:23–24 NIV).

First, notice that you are to take the initiative to repair any rift in your marriage relationship. If you know your spouse is offended or hurt, go deal with it. In fact, the very next verse says, "settle matters quickly." Whatever is injuring your marriage, fix it quickly. Do not let it fester. Do not let it grow. Do not let it worsen. If you ignore it or let it go, the problem will only get worse. The anger and bitterness will hang around so settle things quickly.

I hope you will heed the advice today from God's Word if indeed you find yourself in conflict with your mate. The Bible says "Where there is strife, there is pride, but wisdom is found in those who take advice" (Proverbs 13:10 NIV). If you do not listen to biblical advice and make changes, you will continue to get the same results.

If you have a great marriage, keep doing what you are doing. If you have a bad marriage, be willing to settle things right now by taking the advice of Jesus to "go and be reconciled" to your spouse.

Chapter 4

Your Extreme Marriage Makeover

*Men, you'll never be a good groom to your wife
unless you're first a good bride to Jesus.*
~Tim Keller

Refresh, Renew, and Revitalize Your Marriage

Enjoy life with your wife, whom you love,
all the days of this meaningless life that
God has given you under the sun—all your
meaningless days. For this is your lot in life
and in your toilsome labor under the sun
(Ecclesiastes 9:9 NIV).

In this final chapter, I want to share a game plan with you to refresh, renew, and revitalize your marriage.

In Ecclesiastes 9:9, Solomon, the wisest man who ever lived, gives us some very important advice, "Now, tomorrow, next week, next month, next year, next decade, enjoy life."

How do you enjoy life? You should enjoy marriage..

Marriage is meant to be enjoyed. When God created Adam and Eve and placed them in the garden, He did not say, "Now, go be bored" or "Go have a fight." No, He told them to be fruitful, multiply, enjoy life, enjoy all of creation, and enjoy each other.

If your marriage is not something you enjoy or if you would like to make your marriage stronger, consider this powerful passage of Scripture which will help you improve your marriage. That passage is found in 1 Corinthians 13.

A number of years ago, Sir Isaac Newton discovered how sunlight through a triangular prism, produced all the colors in the spectrum. In 1 Corinthians 13, Paul shows something similar. God's grace and love seen through a prism unfolds different shades and colors of God's love. Those shades and colors of love are exactly what our love ought to be as we focus on our relationship with our husband or wife.

In the New Testament, there are four separate Greek words for love. The first is *eros*, that is, our emotive or erotic love and passion. You probably had this kind of love when you began to date your spouse. Eros love is not the kind of love that Paul refers to in this passage.

There is another Greek word called *phileo*. We get our words *Philadelphia* and *philosophy* from this. It is brotherly love, the love of friendship, but Paul is not referring to *phileo* love in 1 Corinthians 13.

The third kind of love mentioned in the New Testament is *storge* love. It is the familial love that a parent has for his or her son or daughter or the love that a child has for his or her parent. But Paul is not referring to this type of love either.

Paul writes of *agape* love which is an active and sacrificial love. *Agape* love moves and demonstrates itself through actions. In fact, each time love is mentioned in 1 Corinthians 13, it is a verb, not a noun. In the original language, every mention of love is a verb, which means action. Love practices patience, kindness, and self-control. When applied to marriage, *agape* love is not something you get it is something you do. Accordingly, marriage is not a noun, it is a verb filled with loving action. Tim Keller put love's action in marriage this way, "In sharp contrast with our culture, the Bible teaches that the essence of marriage is a sacrificial commitment to the good of the other. That means that love is more fundamentally *action* than *emotion*."

A popular television show is *Extreme Makeover: Home Edition*. In every episode, the designers make plans for their contractors and volunteers to execute. They do more than think about how they can help the family who needs a new home; they work and build that new home.

Deep down, I believe every husband and wife want to love their spouse better. They create a plan and have every intention of acting on that plan—until their spouse says something that disrupts or derails the plan. If you want to transform your marriage, put a plan into practice. The beginning of your plan is to practice God's love.

So let me give you a plan of action based on 1 Corinthians 13. I pray you will act on it today.

Loving Communication

In verse one of 1 Corinthians 13, Paul says, *"If I speak in the tongues of men or of angels, but do not have love, I am only a resounding gong or a clanging cymbal."* Loving communication is the way to remake your marriage. As a pastor, I am disheartened when I meet with people who know about God's grace, God's love, and God's Word, but speak to their spouses in insulting or antagonistic ways. It is as if they feel free to step into God's place as righteous judge and condemn their mates for not measuring up to their personal standards.

Paul says that you can fill yourself up with all the spiritual knowledge in the world, but what reveals your heart is the way you speak to others. Men, do not devalue or discount your brides with your words. Women, do not undercut or speak dismissively about your husband among friends or your children. Paul says love through communication. That means ladies might tell their husbands, "You are handsome. You look great in that." Guys say the same things to their wives. "Babe, you are beautiful."

But more than this, loving communication offers the benefit of the doubt, listens to the other point of view, and respects others even in disagreement. It is unloving to demonize those with whom you disagree. Saying, "If you hadn't done this, I wouldn't be saying this

57

to you" is just a cover up for not speaking in love. The latter part of that phrase acknowledges that what is being said is, in fact, unloving. Respect each other's thoughts, education, and experience, so that even when you disagree passionately about an issue, you still speak to each other with obvious love.

Kind-Hearted Consideration

Starting in verse four, Paul describes active love. *"Love is patient, love is kind. It does not envy, it does not boast, it is not proud."* How should these be translated from the original language? "Love practices being patient. Love practices being kind. Love practices not envying. Love practices not boasting. Love practices not being proud." In other words, you have to make a predetermined decision to practice each one of these facets of love.

Practice being patient. You practiced patience when you started dating. If she was a little late, it did not matter. Now that you have been married a while, you are impatient with her tardiness. Paul says to keep on practicing the patience you showed when you were dating no matter how long you have been married.

Practice being kind. Do you want to transform the heart of your spouse? Seek out new ways to show the same kindness you did when you were dating without expecting something in return.

Perhaps, over the years, you have developed an adversarial relationship with your husband or wife. It can and does happen. Far too often, I see it when I counsel couples. When they come in, they enter with arms crossed in a combative mode. They are no longer working together or demonstrating the basics of kind-hearted consideration, instead they are constantly fighting. I try to show the couple how everything would change if they would begin to practice kindness. "Be completely humble and gentle; be patient, bearing with one another in love. Make every effort to keep the unity of the Spirit through the bond of peace" (Ephesians 4:2–3 NIV). In other words, acknowledge you are not the perfect husband or the perfect wife. If you want to remake your marriage, it is going to take kind-hearted energy. Renewal will happen because you love each other enough to come together to make every effort to transform your communication, to practice consideration and kindness.

If you and your mate are believers in Christ, if the Spirit of God lives within you both, then you will be at peace with one another if you follow the Spirit's lead. The Holy Spirit will not conflict with himself, so if the two of you focus on Jesus and living under the direction of God's Spirit, you will live in harmony. Any conflicts you have started began in the flesh. When everything is about what "I" want, you have no room for what others want. Instead, consider each other kind-heartedly. Chances are the Spirit is already prompting you as to how you can and should be more kind-hearted, the only question is will you practice what you know to be the right actions.

A Willing Compromise

If you want to revitalize your marriage, live a life of willing compromise. Men, you may join your wife at an event or place where you have little interest. But when she asks, "Are you having a good time?" reply, "I am with you, and with you is where I want to be." That is a willing compromise.

Love "does not dishonor others, it is not self-seeking, it is not easily angered, it keeps no record of wrongs" (1 Corinthians 13:5 NIV). Love practices not being rude or dishonoring your mate. Sometimes our best choice is to bite our lip and when we don't bite our lip learn to say, "I am sorry."

Love does not seek itself. Unselfishness is the essence of a willing compromise, but unselfishness takes practice. I have four kids, and I have never needed to train one of them to be selfish. Selfishness is like a wild horse. If you don't keep the reins pulled tight, selfishness will run wild in every relationship you have.

Too often, we practiced being unselfish and the art of compromise before we got married. Then, over time, we stopped looking out for each other and began to loosen up the reins of selfishness, allowing that wild horse to run ahead and destroy our relationship. A 1 Corinthian 13 lover practices not being easily angered and the only way to keep from being easily angered is to stay unselfish. You cannot willingly compromise if you are easily angered. You cannot predetermine in your heart that if your spouse does a certain thing again, you will be angry. Instead, practice extending grace and restrain selfishness.

Paul's last advice in verse five is to reject keeping any record of wrongs. Live as though your marriage is a whiteboard. Be quick to erase any actions by your spouse that irritate and anger you. Erasing enables us to practice willing compromise and will refresh our marriages.

Consistent Fidelity

> *Jesus' teaching in general implies that happy and fulfilling sexual relations in marriage depend on each partner aiming to give satisfaction to the other. If it is the joy of each to make the other happy, a hundred problems will be solved before they happen.*
> ~John Piper

Remove all doubt in your spouse's mind that you could or would ever be unfaithful, especially if you travel a lot for business. Put guards up so you won't be tempted. Make sure your spouse knows that he or she is the only one for you.

"Love does not delight in evil but rejoices with the truth" (1 Corinthians 13:6 NIV). If you work in an office with, someone who seems too available to help you or who suggests private social meetings, run. Never delight in evil, even a little bit of evil. You might think it will never go anywhere, but if you find yourself trying to hide anything from your spouse, then you are probably taking the first steps to delighting in evil. Avoid it. The literal translation of this verse is something like this: "Love practices rejecting any thoughts, words or actions of evil intent," therefore, if there is any evil intent in a relationship outside of marriage, reject it completely!

Instead, Paul says to rejoice in the truth. The truth is this: The sweetest and best marriage you will ever have is the one you are in right now. As Solomon, the wisest man who ever lived, said in Proverbs 5:18–19, "May your fountain be blessed, and may you rejoice in the wife of your youth… May you ever be intoxicated with her love." When you are intoxicated with anything, it changes your speech, thoughts, and actions. Solomon says be intoxicated with only one drink—your mate!

Take an internal inventory, asking what draws your thoughts away from you being intoxicated with your mate. Co-workers? Television viewing? Internet browsing? Something else?
As I researched material for this book, I came across a number of articles about how pornography destroys homes. Someone may say that it is no big deal to look, but it is a big deal because pornography will wreck your home just like an affair will. It will cause you to be distant from and discouraged with your mate. Your wife needs to know that she is all you ever think about, so practice fidelity to her. Wives your husband needs to know that he is the man of your dreams. Practice fidelity to him.

An Enduring Commitment

God intends and expects marriage to be a lifetime commitment between a man and a woman, based on the principles of biblical love. The relationship between Jesus Christ and His church is the supreme example of the committed love that a husband and wife are to follow in their relationship with each other.
~John C. Broger

Hollywood and high profile couples are notorious for signing prenuptial agreements. These agreements essentially say "when our marriage is over and we want to move on, we can still have what is ours." I often wonder, *Why did you bother getting married?* Marriage is about two becoming one in every aspect of life—physically, financially, and emotionally.

I am far more concerned about the unspoken post-nuptial agreements many Christian couples put into effect after they get married. During the ceremony, the bride and groom say, "I love you for better, for worse, for richer, for poorer, till death do us part." But after they have been married for a while, the vow morphs into, *I will love you, if you will just do this or do that to make me happy.*

Love, God's *agape* love, never fails. Love "bears all things, believes all things, hopes all things, endures all things" (1 Corinthians 13:7 NASB).

Agape love **bears all things**. The root of the Greek word for *bears* is roof. *Agape* love is like a roof protecting those we love. A husband is a roof over his family and his wife. Love protects all things in his care. A wife is the covering, providing grace and kindness, over the family and her husband.

Agape love **believes all things.** This phrase is an encouragement to believe the best about anyone and every action. This is the spirit of the optimist and not the pessimist. It thinks the best and not the worst. One person said the idea behind this phrase is to be "easily persuaded" to believe the best about the other or to give grace for an unintended harm.

If you have been hurt in the past, believing the best can be hard to do. However, Paul encourages you to trust your mate and give him or her the benefit of the doubt. Believe until the undisputed facts come out. In doing so, you will foster trust in the heart of your spouse with communication and concern. This doesn't mean that we ignore warning signs of something going wrong, but it does mean to believe the best when facts are in question or unclear. When you trust, when you "believe all things," you believe that God wants to put you together and that God wants to put you together in a powerful union that will be the sweetest relationship you have ever known. That is what God desires; believe Him.

Agape love **hopes all things.** There are times in your relationship when all you will have is hope. "For richer and for poorer," and you are on the poorer side of richer. "For better, for worse," and you are on the worse side of better. "In sickness and in health," and you are on the sickness side of health. In those times, all you can do is hope that God will keep your marriage sweet and fresh. This kind of hope believes that somehow and some way things will turn out OK. This is the kind of hope that would quote "we know that in all things God works for the good of those who love him, who have been called according to his purpose"(Romans 8:28 NIV). That is a heavenly hope—that God can still work everything out for the good.

Agape love **endures all things**. Enduring is difficult and in the context of *agape* love, we are to bear up under hardship and persecution from others. No doubt, if your mate is unfaithful you are the one that has to endure the consequences and pain that comes along with that unfaithfulness. The simple answer would be to simply say I'm out of here. However, Paul said to hang in there and endure it until there is clearly no hope of redemption. In other words, don't quit before the game is over regardless of the score. Instead, leave room for God to work a miracle comeback. Peter said, "Above all, love each other deeply, because love covers over a multitude of sins" (1 Peter 4:8 NIV). An enduring commitment loves so deeply that you are able to look beyond the failures of your spouse.

Today, if you feel like your marriage needs an extreme makeover, consider these questions.

Do you desire to makeover your marriage?

If you desire to makeover your marriage, will you commit to making changes and acting on the desire to change?

Will you be dedicated to improving your marriage? Will you never give up when the makeover requires hard work? Will you continue to rebuild your relationship until the remodel is complete and your relationship is new, different, and more beautiful than before?

Make Your Marriage Last

There is no more lovely, friendly or charming relationship, communion or company, than a good marriage. ~Martin Luther

If you follow the outline in this book, you will begin a joyful makeover with your mate. God's design is for your marriage to last.

Acknowledge that the differences that once pulled us toward our mate can repel us if we are not careful. For some, the makeover will not be that extreme. A little paint here and a little putty there and your marriage will be back on track. For other couples, the work will be much more taxing and difficult, but if—and the key word is *if*—you are willing to put in the work, your marriage can and will sizzle again. Regardless of where you are in your marriage, I believe the end result is always worth it—a marriage that did not melt down but stood strong!

About the Author

John Mark is the Senior Pastor of the thriving Cottonwood Creek Church in Allen, Texas, where he has served since 1995. John Mark earned a Bachelor of Business Administration degree from Baylor University in 1987, a Master of Theology from Criswell College, and a Master of Divinity with Biblical Languages degree from Southwestern Baptist Theological Seminary. He received his Ph.D. from Southwestern Baptist Theological Seminary in 2001. John Mark has written numerous publications on Pastoral Leadership, Ministry Ethics, Marriage, Family, Apologetics, and assorted other topics. He writes and records a daily radio message. John Mark's blog page, www.johnmarkcaton.com archives these messages as well as current hot topics and sermon series.

John Mark and his wife, Jeana, grew up together near Houston, Texas, and they have been married since 1990. They have four children—Jace, Jordan, Jensyn and Jarrett. The Catons reside in Allen, Texas.

Follow John Mark @

Facebook: community page-
https://www.facebook.com/johnmark.caton
or
Facebook: public page
https://www.facebook.com/johnmark.caton

Twitter: @JohnMarkCaton

Instagram: pastorjohnmark

Blog: johnmarkcaton.com